Blessed from above

(A Jesusbride Collection)

Author: Olubukayo Oladunjoye

DEDICATION

I dedicate this prayer memoir of to my mother, Mrs. Aderonke Oyetayo, a woman of inestimable value and a beacon of hope.

Introduction

In life's journey there often comes phases where we become clueless on how to forge ahead. These may be difficult moments, tough seasons, challenging periods of discomfort, untoward happenings and unprecedented patterns. Some describe this as life crisis, some may describe this phase as walking under closed heavens, groping in the dark. When all hope seems lost and acquired wit fails, what do we do?

This work 'Blessed from above' presents the power of heartfelt blessings and prayers for realization of our desired change. Do you remember the prayer of Hannah, the prayer of Jabesh, and the prayer of the Lord Jesus in the Garden of Gethsemane? In this times Mrs. Olubukayo Oladunjoye shares tested and proven prayers, accompanied with pictoral illustrations to aid the user's imagination and engagement. May your petitions be granted as you pray along.

And they helped David against the band of the rovers: for they were all mighty men of valour, and were captains in the host.

For at that time day by day there came to David to help him, until it was a great host, like the host of God.

1 Chronicles 12 vs 21 - KJV

Prayer: *Please send daily helpers to me as you sent to David.*

Also thou shalt lie down, and none shall make thee afraid; yea, many shall make suit unto thee

Job 11 vs 19 KJV

Day 2: ___/ ___/ ___

Prayer: May I dwell in peace and safety.

But be ye glad and rejoice for ever in that which I create: for, behold, I create Jerusalem a rejoicing, and her people a joy.

Isaiah 65:18 KJV

Day 3: ___/ ___/ ___

Prayer: Make me a delight and my people a joy.

For Zion's sake will I not hold my peace, and for Jerusalem's sake I will not rest, until the righteousness thereof go forth as brightness, and the salvation thereof as a lamp that burneth

Isaiah 62 vs 1 KJV

Prayer: Let my righteousness shine out like the dawn and my salvation like a blazing torch.

Behold, we count them happy which endure. Ye have heard of the patience of Job, and have seen the end of the Lord; that the Lord is very pitiful, and of tender mercy

James 5 vs 11 KJV

Prayer: The Lord is full of compassion and mercy so I will persevere.

And out of them shall proceed thanksgiving and the voice of them that make merry: and I will multiply them, and they shall not be few; I will also glorify them, and they shall not be small.

Jeremiah 30:19 KJV

Prayer: We shall not be small.

The horse is prepared against the day of battle: but safety is of the Lord

Proverbs 21 vs 31 KJV

Day 7: ___/ ___/ ___

Prayer: I declare that our safety and victory is of the Lord.

14

And the LORD shall make thee the head, and not the tail; and thou shalt be above only, and thou shalt not be beneath; if that thou hearken unto the commandments of the LORD thy God, which I command thee this day, to observe and to do them.

Deuteronomy 28:13 KJV

Prayer: May we be attentive and obedient to faithful instruction always and be elevated.

The heart of her husband doth safely trust in her, so that he shall have no need of spoil

Proverbs 31:11 KJV

Day 9: ___/ ___/ ___

Prayer: We shall lack nothing of value.

I will give you the treasures of darkness and hidden riches of secret places, that you may know that I, the LORD, who call you by your name, am the God of Israel

Isaiah 45 vs 3 KJV

Prayer: As I am called by God, hidden richness and depth will be accessible to me.

And let the beauty of the LORD our God be upon us: and establish thou the work of our hands upon us; yea, the work of our hands establish thou it

Psalm 90 vs 17

Prayer: May God establish the work of our hands for us.

And I will make them and the places round about my hill a blessing; and I will cause the shower to come down in his season; there shall be showers of blessing.

Ezekiel 34:26 KJV

Day 12: ___/ ___/ ___

Prayer: Dear Lord God, please prosper me and my loved ones exceedingly.

And they shall dwell in the land that I have given unto Jacob my servant, wherein your fathers have dwelt; and they shall dwell therein, even they, and their children, and their children's children for ever: and my servant David shall be their prince for ever.

Moreover I will make a covenant of peace with them; it shall be an everlasting covenant with them: and I will place them, and multiply them, and will set my sanctuary in the midst of them for evermore.

My tabernacle also shall be with them: yea, I will be their God, and they shall be my people.

Ezekiel 37:27 KJV

Prayer: May the Lord dwell permanently with us.

Hitherto have ye asked nothing in my name: ask, and ye shall receive, that your joy may be full.

John 16 vs 24 KJV

Prayer: The blessings from Day 1 to 13 and more I ask in the name of Jesus Christ. Amen!

Do you want to share you thoughts with the authors? or provide feedback? please complete the response form via the link:

https://forms.gle/fsKXp2YW446GzXHQA

or scan the QR code below:

Author:
Olubukayo Oladunjoye

Illustrators:
Emmanuella Johnson, Ayomide Adeeko

Graphics design:
Tolulope Folorunso